Scary Creatures
BIG CATS

Written by
Penny Clarke

Illustrated by
Terry Riley

Created and designed by
David Salariya

BOOK HOUSE

Author:

Penny Clarke is an author and editor
specialising in information books for children. The
books she has written include titles on natural history,
rainforests and volcanoes, as well as others on
different periods of history. She used to live in central
London, but thanks to modern technology she has
now realised her dream of being able to live and work
in the countryside.

Artist:

Terry Riley worked for many years as an art
director in advertising before writing and illustrating
his own series of children's books. He is passionate
about natural history and has illustrated hundreds of
wildlife projects for publishing, film and television.

Additional artists:
Mark Bergin
Robert Morton
Carolyn Scrace
David Stewart

Series creator:

David Salariya was born in Dundee,
Scotland. In 1989 he established The Salariya Book
Company. He has illustrated a wide range of books
and has created many new series for publishers in the
UK and overseas. He lives in Brighton with his wife,
illustrator Shirley Willis, and their son.

Consultant:

Dr Gerald Legg holds a doctorate in zoology
from Manchester University. He worked in West Africa for
several years as a lecturer and rainforest researcher and
his current position is biologist at the Booth Museum of
Natural History in Brighton. He is also the author of many
natural history books for children.

Editor: Karen Barker Smith

Picture research: Nicky Roe

Published in Great Britain in 2003 by
Book House, an imprint of
The Salariya Book Company Ltd
25 Marlborough Place, Brighton BN1 1UB

Visit the Salariya Book Company at
www.salariya.com
www.book-house.co.uk

A catalogue record for this book is available
from the British Library.

HB ISBN: 978-1-904194-40-8
PB ISBN: 978-1-904194-41-5

Printed in Hong Kong.
Printed on paper from sustainable forests.
Reprinted in 2008.

Photographic credits:

Corbis Images: 18, 19
John Foxx Images: 5, 13, 15, 16, 17, 21
T Kitchin & V Hurst, NHPA: 10
PhotoDisc: 11
Christophe Ratier, NHPA: 12
RSPCA: 29
Kevin Schafer, NHPA: 22

Contents

What is a big cat?

There are about 35 species of wild cat. They are all carnivores and hunt and catch their food. The six largest species are known as the 'big cats'. These are the lion, tiger, jaguar, leopard, cheetah and snow leopard. But some experts disagree with this. They argue that the true big cats are only those that roar. If they are right, only the lion, tiger, leopard and jaguar are truly big cats.

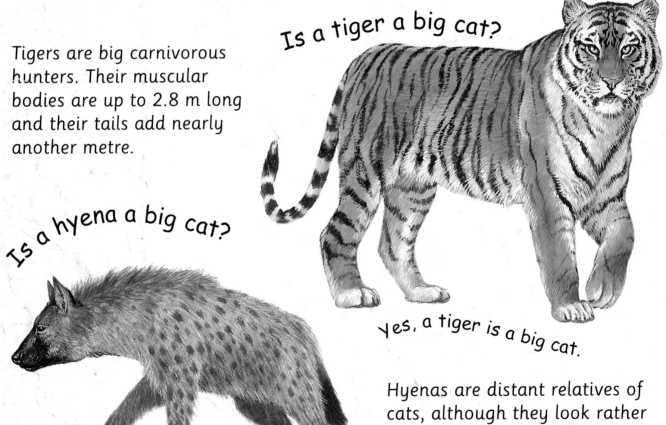

Tigers are big carnivorous hunters. Their muscular bodies are up to 2.8 m long and their tails add nearly another metre.

Is a tiger a big cat?

Is a hyena a big cat?

Yes, a tiger is a big cat.

No, a hyena is not a big cat.

Hyenas are distant relatives of cats, although they look rather like dogs. They are good hunters – a pack of spotted hyenas can kill a zebra – but they are also scavengers and eat carrion.

A panther – a type of leopard

Why are big cats scary?

An adult lion's body is about 2 m long even without the tail. Perhaps it is this large size that makes such big cats scary. Most big cats can roar very loudly and this can be frightening. We know that big cats are faster and stronger than humans. Apart from a gun, we have no defence against a hungry big cat.

How do claws work?

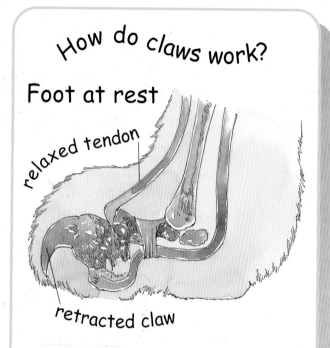

Foot at rest

relaxed tendon

retracted claw

Claws in use

contracted tendon

extended claw

All cats have long, sharp, retractile claws. They use them to grasp prey and grip tree trunks when they climb. When cats are not grasping or climbing they retract their claws within their footpads. The cheetah is the only cat that cannot do this.

X-Ray Vision

Hold the page opposite up to the light and see what's inside a lion.

See what's inside

hairy mane

large paws

long tail for balance

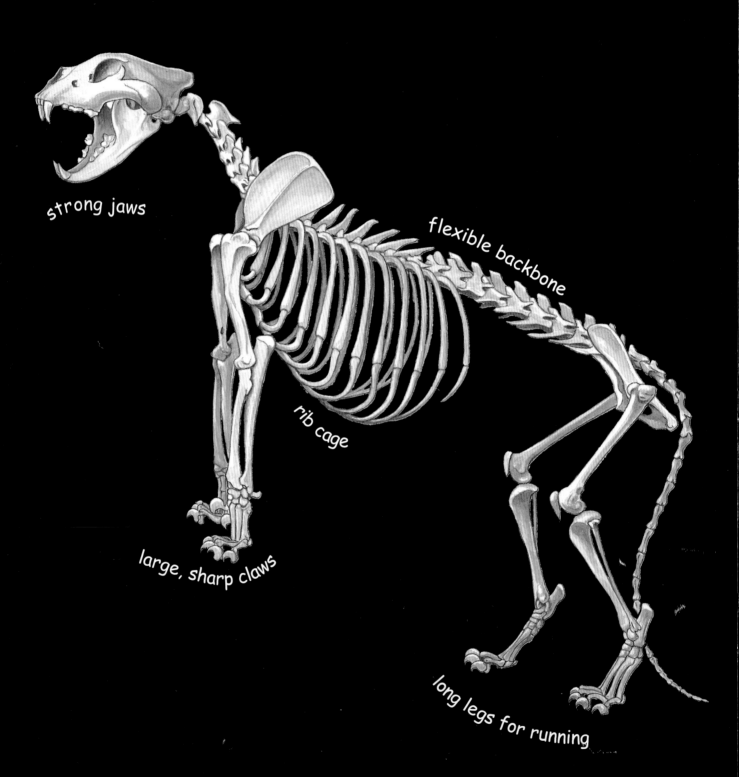

What's inside a big cat?

All cats, whatever their size, have bodies perfect for hunting. They have broad rib cages so there is plenty of room for their lungs. They need to breathe fast when they are running at speed. Their flexible backbones help them twist and turn as they chase after their prey.

Big cats have powerful jaws so they can kill with a single bite to the neck. If they don't kill instantly their prey might escape.

Human

Leopard

Leopards are smaller than lions and tigers, but are still larger and more powerful than any human. Like most big cats, the males and females are the same size: about 1.9 m long with tails of nearly 1.4 m.

Cats are hunters. They kill with a bite of their long dagger-like canine teeth. When they eat, they tear through flesh with their carnassial teeth (right).

canine teeth

carnassial teeth

Skull of a leopard

What do big cats eat?

Big cats are carnivores – they eat other living creatures. The bigger the big cat, the bigger its prey. Lions will hunt buffalo and giraffes, which are much bigger than they are. Tigers hunt gaurs, which are large wild relatives of cows. If their normal prey is hard to find, big cats will eat small animals like mice and hares. Leopards will even scavenge meat they have not caught themselves.

Did you know?

The mountain lion lives on the American continent, from Canada in the north to the mountains of South America. It is also called the puma, silver lion and cougar. Its food ranges from large mule deer to small snowshoe hares.

Mountain lion with its prey – a snowshoe hare

Male lion killing a zebra

Lions live in groups. After they have killed, members of the group gather to eat the prey. The cubs are not allowed to eat before the adults. Leopards live alone and when they kill large prey they drag it up a tree so they can eat it without hyenas or vultures trying to grab it.

wildebeest

antelope

baboon

hare

boar

zebra

deer   dog

Big cat prey

Do all big cats hunt?

Snow leopards live in the Himalayas and the mountains of Russia and northern Asia. They hunt mountain animals like ibex and boar, as well as ground-nesting birds.

Lions and leopards hunt antelope and zebras, and leopards also hunt baboons. In winter, the snowshoe hares hunted by mountain lions turn white, to match the snow covering the ground. This makes hunting them more difficult.

Jaguars, which live mostly in Central and South America, hunt tapirs, deer, otters and even turtles and caiman.

Yes, all big cats hunt.

Are big cats good hunters?

Big cats are the best hunters in the world. Their flexible, muscular bodies, excellent eyesight and speed make it difficult for their prey to escape. Lions and jaguars are not as fast as the other big cats, but make up for this in other ways. Lions often hunt in a group and jaguars are superb stalkers.

Did you know?

Cheetahs are the fastest of the big cats. They watch their prey from long grass, then slowly stalk it before leaping out and running it down. As cheetahs run, at speeds of up to 112 kph, their long tail helps them keep their balance.

12 Cheetah chasing a gazelle

Leopard preparing to pounce on its prey

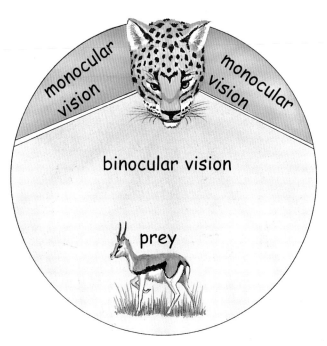

Big cat eyesight

Big cats' large, forward-looking eyes give them binocular vision (left), just like humans. This means they can judge distances accurately, which is essential for successful hunting.

Most big cats stalk their prey, although leopards will often drop on their victims from a tree (above). A stalk begins with the big cat downwind of its prey. That means the cat's scent is blown away from the animal it is hunting. If the hunted animal smelt the cat it would be off in a flash. The cat creeps forward, often on its stomach. Then, when it is very close, it pounces or gives chase.

When a cheetah runs it stretches its spine as it leaps through the air and bounds along.

How fast can big cats run?

A cheetah can run extremely fast, reaching a speed of 112 kph. When it gets to its prey it knocks it sideways, then kills it by biting its throat. But a cheetah is a sprinter, not a long-distance runner. If it does not catch its prey quickly it gives up the chase. If the cheetah continued it would just be a waste of energy because the prey would escape as the cheetah slowed down.

Can cheetahs run faster than lions?

The cheetah is fast because it has a slender, streamlined body. Compare the pictures on this page with those of the tiger on page 4 and the lion on page 7. The cheetah's long legs and a flexible spine also help.

Yes, cheetahs are the fastest big cats.

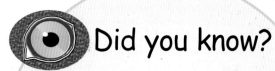 Did you know?

Cheetahs cannot run at top speed for more than about 550 m. Sometimes a cheetah family group works together, taking it in turns to chase and exhaust animals such as zebras which can run fast for great distances.

Do cheetahs stalk their prey?

Cheetahs live in the open grasslands of Africa called savannahs. In the savannah there are few trees and bushes for cheetahs to hide in while hunting. Instead they have to crouch and stalk through the long grass before making a final dash across open ground to their prey.

Yes, cheetahs stalk their prey.

Cheetah walking on the savannah

Why do leopards have spots?

Leopards have spots for camouflage. Camouflage is a type of disguise – it makes something difficult to see. The spots and patterns on big cats' coats break up their outline, helping them to blend in with their surroundings (below). This makes them even more difficult for their prey to see.

Why do tigers have stripes?

Tigers live in forests and woodland. Sunlight shining through the trees makes shadows on the ground. The tiger's dark stripes look like shadows. They break up the outline of its body, helping to camouflage it as it stalks its prey among the trees.

Tigers' stripes are for camouflage.

Cheetah camouflaged in long grass

Did you know?

Lions' coats range in colour from a pale yellow-brown to a rich reddish-brown. These colours help them blend in with the dry grasslands of southern Africa where they live. Only male lions have manes (above). The mane helps make the lion look even larger and fiercer.

Male lion

17

Are big cats good parents?

Female big cats are excellent mothers. They will attack anything that threatens their cubs. Most big cats are solitary, so the cubs are reared just by their mother. In fact, the female will attack and drive away the cubs' father if he comes near them.

Did you know?

Lions are the only big cats to live in groups. Each group, or pride, is usually made up of about three adult males, 15 females and their cubs. When the male cubs are about 18 months old they are driven away to find a territory and a mate for themselves.

Lioness with her cubs

Young cheetahs with their mother

Do cubs stay with their mother?

Most big cat cubs will stay with their mother until they are between 18 months and two years old.

Tiger cubs are with their mothers for several years. Like all mammals, tiger cubs feed on their mothers' milk for the first few months. Then she starts bringing them food she has caught. By the time they are six months old the cubs begin hunting with their mother. Gradually they learn the skills they will need to survive when they leave her care.

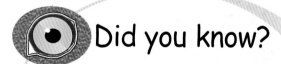 Did you know?

Leopards often give birth to their cubs in a hole in a tree, where they will be safe when their mother goes out hunting.

Yes, most big cat cubs stay with their mother until they are fully grown.

Do big cats live in cold places?

We think of lions and cheetahs hunting zebras and antelope in the hot grasslands of southern Africa, where leopards sun themselves on tree branches. But the snow leopard lives high in the Himalayas. In summer it hunts birds, mountain sheep and goats among the glaciers and snowfields. In winter it follows its prey down to the lower slopes, about 2,000 m above sea level.

 Did you know?

Snow leopard cubs start hunting with their mothers at two months old – younger than other big cat cubs. Food is difficult to find where they live, so each snow leopard has to cover long distances, too far for the mother to return to her cubs each time.

The snow leopard has thick, beautiful fur to keep it warm. Sadly, it is now rare because it has been hunted for its fur.

Snow leopard

Tiger wading into a river to keep cool

Do tigers like lying in the sun?

Most big cats love lying in the sun. Tigers do not. Millions of years ago tigers lived in areas of Asia with long cold winters. Today, most wild tigers live in the forests of India where the summers are hot. To keep cool they lie in water, especially at midday when it is hottest. If there is no water nearby, they lie in the deepest shade they can find.

No, tigers prefer to lie in the shade.

Tigers used to live throughout much of Asia, from Siberia in the north to Bali in the south. Each region had its own variety of tiger, called a subspecies. The biggest difference between each subspecies was the colour and thickness of its coat. Many of these subspecies are now extinct.

Do big cats have small relatives?

Most species of cat are less than a metre long. They are much smaller than the big cats, but they look very similar. They all have strong muscular bodies. Their heads are short and broad, their eyes are large and they have lots of whiskers around their nose and mouth. Most of them also have long tails.

X-Ray Vision

Hold the page opposite up to the light and see what's inside a domestic cat.

See what's inside

Unlike most cats bobcats have short tails – less than 20 cm long. Bobcats live in forests, woods, swamps and grasslands in western North America and Mexico. They stalk their prey slowly before pouncing and killing it with a bite – just like domestic cats.

North American bobcat in winter

Domestic cats are as good at hunting as their wild relations. They kill vermin such as mice and rats, but also kill millions of garden birds each year.

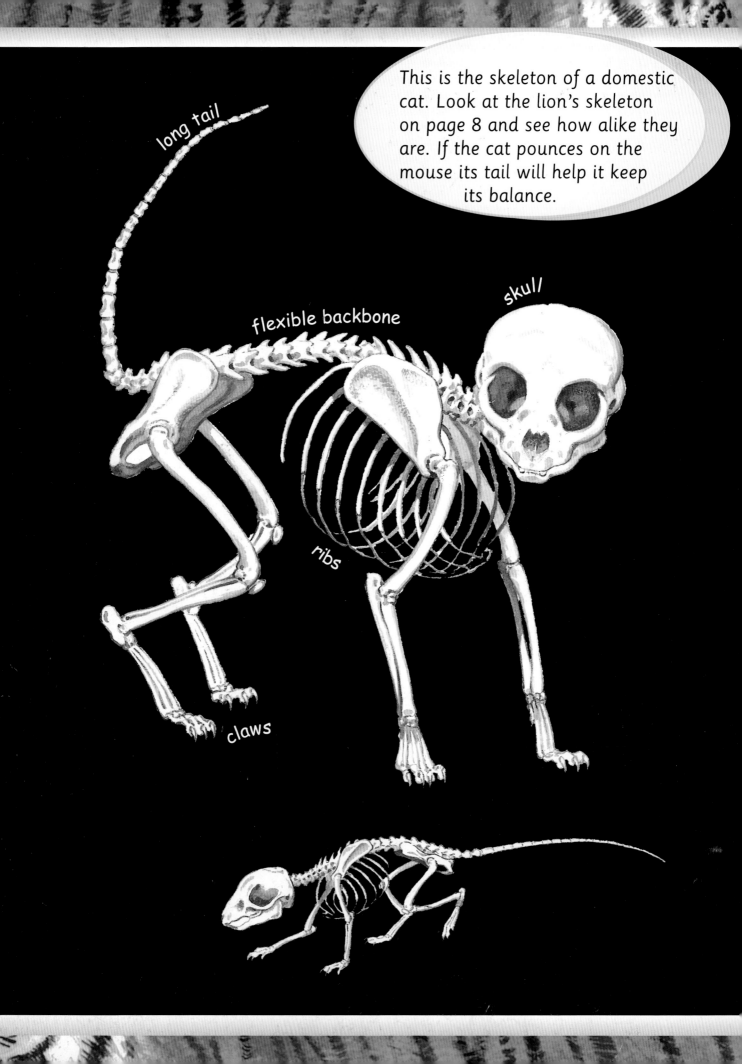

What do other cats look like?

Wild cats need good camouflage for hunting, so the colour of their fur varies according to where they live. For example, when the pampas cats of South America live in forests their coats are darker than when they live in sunny open grasslands.

Servals (below) live in the woods and plains of southern Africa. Their fur varies enormously. Servals with light brown coats usually have rows of large black spots. Those with darker coats have small spots dotted all over their body.

Did you know?

A few leopards have no camouflage. They have completely black coats and are called panthers (see page 5).

Serval

The caracal (right) is easy to identify. Its long ears with tufts of dark hair at the tips are quite different from those of any other cat.

Caracal

Where do big cats live?

Different species of cat live all over the world and in all types of climate. The true big cats, however, now live only in South America, Asia and Africa.

Big cats need big prey and the animals they hunt now only live in parts of the world with plenty of space and not too many humans.

Mountain lion

No big cats live in North America. The mountain lion, or cougar, is the largest wild cat there.

Jaguars lived in North America until the early 20th century. They are now an endangered species and can only be found in parts of South America.

Jaguar

Lion

Snow leopard

Tiger

Leopard

Cheetah

What are big cats afraid of?

Big cats have no natural enemies, they are too big and powerful for other animals to hunt. Before the invention of guns they were safe from humans. Guns changed that, as did the world's ever-increasing human population. As forests are cut down to provide timber and land for farming, there is less space for the big cats and their prey.

No one knows how many tigers there are, but there are probably fewer than 1,000 left in the wild.

Did you know?

These animals (below) have been killed just for their skins, for use as rugs or for coats. It takes the skins of several big cats to make a fur coat, bringing some big cats closer to extinction.

Animal skins confiscated by customs officers

Big cat facts

Tigers are nocturnal, which means they hunt at night. Their eyes are adapted to take in as much light as possible so they can see their prey in the dark. A domestic cat's eyes work in the same way.

The heaviest known Indian tiger weighed 389 kg.

The lynx, a relative of the big cats, lives in the mountains of Spain and Portugal as well in colder northern lands. Its tufted ears and cheeks and very short tail make it easy to recognise.

The heaviest known lion weighed 313 kg when it died.

The cheetah is the fastest land mammal over short distances – 112 kph for 550 m. The fastest land mammal over long distances is the pronghorn antelope – 67 kph for 1.6 km, but a cheetah could never catch a pronghorn. Why? Pronghorns live in North America and cheetahs in southern Africa!

The lion is often called the king of the beasts and kings have often used lions on their flags and coats-of-arms to symbolise their own power and strength.

Many tigers are killed each year so parts of their bodies can be used to make traditional medicines in the Far East. There is no scientific evidence that these 'medicines' work.

Lions were hunted in Europe and north Africa by the Romans. Gladiators fighting with lions in the Colosseum in ancient Rome was a very popular entertainment.

Snow leopards are probably the best jumpers of the big cats. In the mountains where they live there are many deep ravines and leaping them is the best way to get across.

Glossary

adapted Something that is suitable for a particular purpose.

binocular vision The ability to see the same area with both eyes at the same time.

caiman A South American relative of crocodiles and alligators.

camouflage Colouring which helps an animal blend in with its surroundings.

carnivore Any animal that eats the flesh of other animals as its main food.

carrion Decaying flesh.

extinct Species of animals that are no longer alive anywhere in the world.

mammal An animal that feeds on its mother's milk when it is a baby.

monocular vision The ability of each eye to see a different area at the same time.

nocturnal An animal that is active at night.

predator Any animal that hunts other living creatures for food.

prey Any animal that is hunted by other animals for food.

retractile Claws which can be extended or withdrawn (retracted) into sheaths, like the claws of cats.

scavenger An animal that eats carrion.

solitary An animal that prefers to live alone.

species A group of living things that look alike, behave in the same way and can interbreed.

subspecies A group of animals in a species that is slightly different from the rest of the species. This is usually because the animals of the subspecies have been isolated from the rest of the species for a long time. For example, the tigers in Siberia are obviously tigers, but look different to those that live in India.

31

Index

I Wonder Why

Pyramids Were Built

and Other Questions About Ancient Egypt

Philip Steele

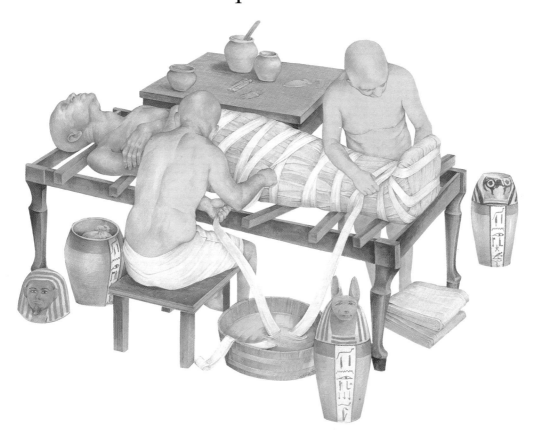

TED SMART

KINGFISHER
Kingfisher Publications Plc
New Penderel House, 283–288 High Holborn,
London WC1V 7HZ

First published by Kingfisher Publications Plc 1995
ISBN 1 85613 592 6

1BP/0899/WKT/HBM(HBM)/157HIQ

This edition published in 1999 for The Book People Ltd,
Hall Wood Avenue, Haydock, St Helens WA11 9UL

Copyright © Kingfisher Publications Plc 1995

Phototypeset by Tradespools Ltd, Frome, Somerset
Printed in China

Series editor: Jackie Gaff
Series designer: David West Children's Books
Author: Philip Steele
Consultant: Department of Egyptian Antiquities,
    British Museum
Editor: Claire Llewellyn, Clare Oliver
Art editor: Christina Fraser
Cover illustrations: Chris Forsey, cartoons by
    Tony Kenyon (B.L. Kearley)
Illustrations: Simone Boni (Virgil Pomfret Agency) 16–17;
    Peter Dennis (Linda Rogers Associates) 14–15, 24–25,
    28–29 ; Chris Forsey 12–13; Luigi Galante (Virgil Pomfret
    Agency) 4–5; Nick Harris (Virgil Pomfret Agency) 18–19,
    22–23; Adam Hook (Linden Artists) 8–9, 26–27, 30–31;
    Tony Kenyon (B.L. Kearley) all cartoons; Nicki Palin 6–7,
    10–11, 20–21.

CONTENTS

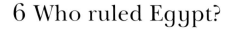

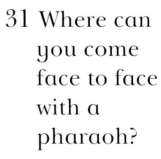

Why do we call Egyptians ancient?

Egypt — AFRICA

We call the Egyptians ancient because they lived such a long time ago – not because they all reached a ripe old age! The first Egyptians were farmers about 8,000 years ago. Within a few thousand years, Egypt had become one of the most powerful countries in the world.

● Will people be studying us in 5,000 years' time? What will they think about the way we live now?

● The Egyptians usually built tombs for dead kings on the river's western bank, where the Sun sets. They believed that their kings went to meet the Sun god when they died.

● Egypt is mostly sandy desert, where nothing grows. The Ancient Egyptians settled on the banks of the river Nile, where there was plenty of water for themselves and their crops.

● The Ancient Egyptians didn't know about distant parts of the world. But they did explore parts of Asia and Africa. And their merchants bought wood, gold, ivory, spices and even apes from nearby countries.

Why were the Egyptians great?

The Egyptians were so good at farming that they became very rich. They built fantastic temples for their gods, and huge pointed tombs called pyramids where they buried their kings. They had armies and ships and courts of law. Their priests studied the stars and their craftspeople made beautiful things from gold and silver.

Mediterranean Sea

Giza
Memphis
Saqqara

LOWER EGYPT

Red Sea

Abydos
Valley of the Kings
Thebes

UPPER EGYPT

Nile River

☐ Farming land
☐ Desert

Who ruled Egypt?

The king of Egypt was called the pharaoh. The Egyptians believed that their Sun god Re was the first king of Egypt, and that all the pharaohs after him were his relatives. This made the pharaoh very holy – and very powerful! The people thought he was a god on Earth.

● The pharaoh's advisors were called the Honoured Ones. There were all sorts of royal officials, too, with grand names like the Director of Royal Dress and the Keeper of the Royal Wigs.

Could a woman be pharaoh?

Although very few women ruled Egypt, there was a famous pharaoh called Hatshepsut. When her six-year-old nephew came to the throne, Hatshepsut was asked to rule Egypt for him – just until he was a little bit older. But Hatshepsut liked ruling so much that she wouldn't let her nephew take over. He didn't get the chance to rule until he was 30 years old!

● When she was pharaoh, Hatshepsut had to wear the badges of royalty. These included a false beard, made of real hair.

How would you know if you met a pharaoh?

He would be wearing a crown, of course! In fact, pharaohs sometimes wore two crowns at the same time – a white one for Upper Egypt, which was the name for the south of the country, and a red one for Lower Egypt, which was the north.

Who was the crocodile god?

In old paintings and carvings, most Egyptian gods and goddesses have animal heads. The water god, Sebek, was shown as a crocodile. Thoth had the head of a bird called an ibis, while Taweret looked like a hippo! Osiris and Isis were luckier. They were shown as a great king and queen.

● The Egyptians loved to wear lucky charms. Their favourites were scarabs. The scarab beetle was sacred to the Sun god, Re.

● The Ancient Egyptians worshipped as many as 2,000 gods and goddesses!

Thoth, god of learning

Osiris, god of death

Who was the goddess Nut?

Nut was goddess of the heavens and she was usually shown covered in stars. Many gods and goddesses were linked in families. Nut was married to Geb. Isis and Osiris were their children.

● Being a priest was a part-time job. Most only spent 3 months a year at the temple, and lived at home the rest of the time.

● Priests had to wash twice during the day and twice at night, to make themselves clean and pure for the gods.

Taweret, goddess of childbirth and babies

Isis, wife of Osiris

Why did the Egyptians bury their mummies?

A mummy is a dead body which has been dried out so it lasts for thousands of years. The Egyptians believed that the dead travelled to another world, where they needed their bodies. And they didn't want any bits missing!

● Some poorer families had their nearest and dearest mummified, but it was an expensive business. Only the rich could afford a really good send-off.

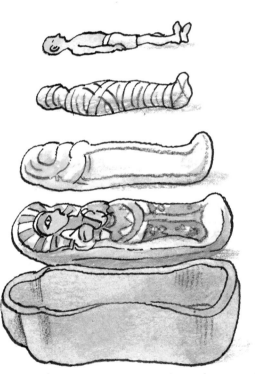

● The mummy was placed inside a series of wooden coffins. These were put in a big stone case called a sarcophagus.

● Monkeys, crocodiles, cats and other sacred animals were often mummified, too!

Why were mummies brainless?

The Ancient Egyptians believed that the heart was the most important part of the whole body. They thought that the brain was useless. So when they were preparing a mummy, they took out the brain – by pulling it down through the nose!

Why were mummies wrapped in bandages?

Wrapping the dead body helped to keep its shape. After the insides were removed, the body was dried out for 40 days in salty stuff called natron. Then it was washed, rubbed with ointments, and tightly bandaged.

Why were the pyramids built?

The pyramids were huge tombs for dead pharaohs and other very important people. No one knows exactly why the pyramids were shaped this way. Some people think they were built to point towards the Sun and stars, so that the dead person's spirit could fly to heaven like a rocket.

● The Great Pyramid at Giza was built more than 4,500 years ago. This is what it looks like today.

● Pharaohs were buried with all their finest clothes and jewellery, so tombs were given sneaky traps to catch out robbers.

● There are other, smaller pyramids at Giza, and over 80 at other places in Egypt. Some have stepped sides and bent tops.

● This is what the Great Pyramid looks like inside.

Pharaoh's chamber

Who liked to get knee-deep in mud?

Egyptian farmers loved mud – it has all the water and goodness that plants need to grow well. The most important time in a farmer's year was when the Nile flooded and dumped rich, black mud on the dry fields. A good flood meant a good harvest. A bad one meant people went hungry.

● Priests watched the Moon and stars to work out a calendar of the months. This told them when the floods would come and when to plant crops.

● Juicy grapes and fresh green vegetables were grown in the rich Nile mud. Golden ears of wheat and barley were harvested and stored in granaries.

● The only farm land in Egypt is near the river Nile. It used to be called the Black Land, because the mud left by the floods was black. The rocky desert was called the Red Land.

Which was the fastest way to travel?

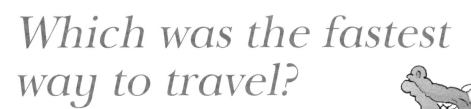

The quickest route in Egypt was the river Nile. Egyptian boats were made from river reeds or wood. They were the only way to get from one side of the river to the other – unless you swam and liked crocodiles!

● The big question each year was: "How deep is the flood?" Notched stones were used like giant rulers to measure the rising water. The stones were called nilometers.

● Farmers dug ditches to carry water to their crops when the Nile wasn't in flood. They used a clever machine called a shaduf to lift water out of the river into the ditches.

Why did people sit on the roof?

The roof was just about the best spot in an Egyptian house. It was cooler than indoors, especially under a shady canopy. People liked to sit and talk there, or play board games.

• Egyptian houses had flat roofs. Pointed roofs were invented in rainy lands, to let the water drain away.

• Most houses were made of mud bricks, but stone blocks were used for temples, tombs and palaces.

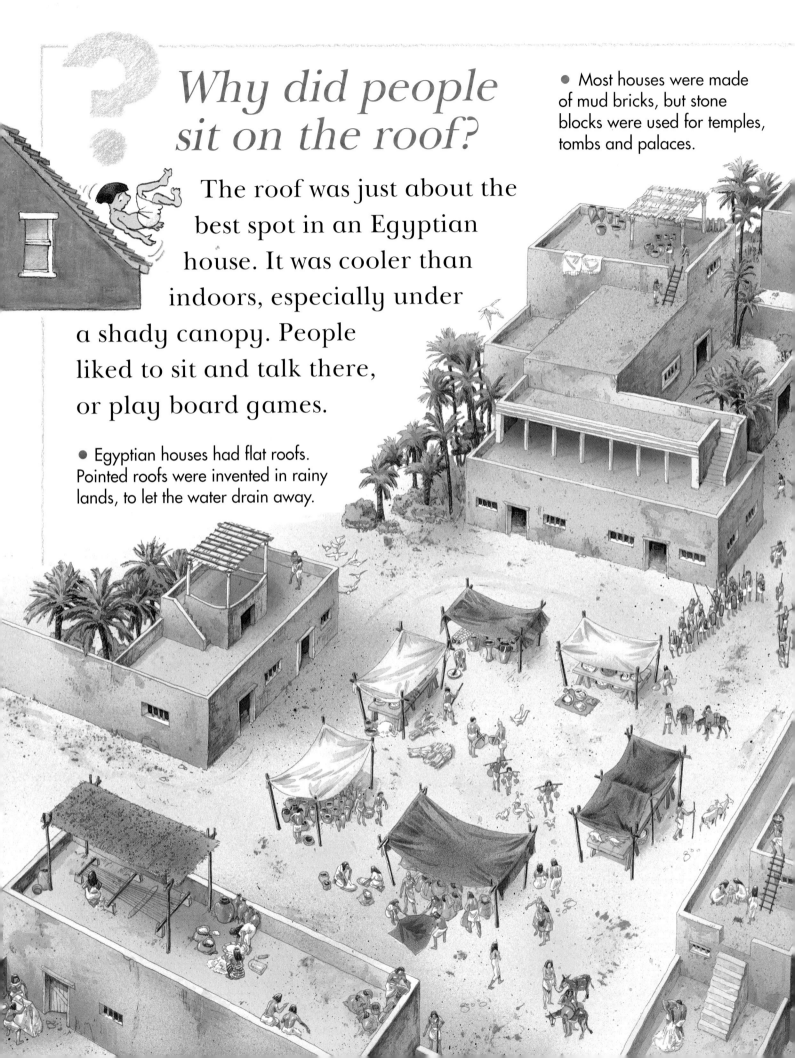

Who made mud pies?

Bricks were made from river mud. Brick-makers trampled the mud with their bare feet until it was sticky. They added bits of straw and reed to make the mixture firmer. Then they shaped the mud pies into bricks, which dried hard in the Sun.

Who had nightmares?

Some Egyptians must have slept well, but their beds do look very uncomfortable! They were made of wood, with ropes or leather straps instead of springs.

And people didn't lie on soft pillows filled with feathers. All they had were wooden headrests!

Who had floury feet?

When Egyptian cooks made bread, they sometimes jumped into a huge bowl on the floor and kneaded the dough with their feet. Let's hope they washed them first!

● Egyptian feet were good at making wine, too. Every last drop of juice was trampled from the grapes.

● The Egyptians baked lots of delicious cakes – ring doughnuts, pyramid-shaped buns, and cakes that looked like crocodiles!

What's the world's stalest bread?

Loaves of bread have been found in Egyptian tombs. No one has tasted them, though. The bread is thousands of years old and as hard as rock!

● Wooden lunch boxes full of meat and fruit were sometimes left in tombs, in case the mummy got hungry in the next world!

● Egyptian bread must have been a bit gritty, even when it was fresh, since many of the mummies' teeth are very worn down.

Who had splendid feasts?

Well, poor people certainly didn't! Pharaohs and rich people held fantastic feasts, where they ate juicy pieces of beef, mutton or goose. The meat was sometimes barbequed, and served with crunchy onions or garlic, as well as spinach, leeks, peas or beans. What was for pudding? Juicy figs, sweet melons or pomegranates.

Who looked really cool?

Egypt is a very hot country, and in ancient times people kept cool by wearing as little as possible. Ordinary workers just wore a simple cloth around their waists. But for the rich, the coolest fashion was graceful clothes made from the finest linen.

● Linen is made from a plant called flax. It's very hard to prepare, but the Egyptians could spin and weave it into lengths of beautifully light and flimsy cloth.

● Acrobats and dancing girls just wore strings of beads!

● Women wore long dresses with shoulder straps. Men wore long kilts that hung in folds. Children often wore nothing at all.

Who liked to sparkle?

Most clothes were plain white, so rich people added colour and sparkle by wearing beautiful jewellery made from gold and colourful precious stones. Sometimes, for a special feast, they wore wide cloth collars decorated with leaves, wildflowers or glass-like beads. Poorer people's jewellery was made from copper and shells.

● Both men and women wore jewellery.

Why did shoes wear out?

Servants' shoes were woven from reeds which they gathered from the river bank. The shoes didn't last long – particularly when the servants had to keep running around after their rich masters and mistresses!

Who loved making up?

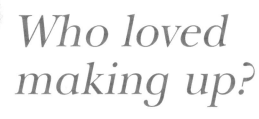

Rich Egyptian women wore lots of striking make-up. Eyeshadow went on first, then a black line around the eyes, and finally a rosy lipstick and cheek blusher. The Ancient Egyptians still look beautiful over 4,000 years later – in their paintings!

Why did women wear cones on their heads?

Rich women pinned cones to their wigs for feasts and parties. But they wore cones of perfumed grease, not ice-cream cones! As the greasy cones melted in the warm evening air, they gave off a sweet perfume.

The Egyptians loved to smell good. Rich people used scented oils and breath fresheners, and they carried sweet-smelling flowers around with them.

● Men liked to look good, so they wore make-up, too.

Who made a beeline for wigs?

Pharaohs and rich people – everybody who was anybody wore a wig on their head. The wigs were made of real hair, which was tied into hundreds of tiny plaits and held in place by sticky beeswax.

● The Egyptians took great care of their looks. They mixed up lotions to stop baldness and dandruff — even spots!

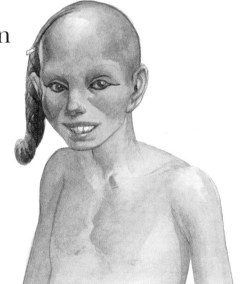

● Young boys' heads were shaved, except for a single plait of hair on the right-hand side.

Who played with lions?

Nobody did, if they had any sense! But young children did play with wooden lions and other toy animals. Children also had spinning tops, as well as balls that rattled, and dolls with beads in their hair.

● Few people could read, so after a day's work they probably sat down to listen to storytellers. There were many exciting tales about gods and goddesses.

● Children ran around playing ball-games or tag, then cooled off with a swim in the river.

24

Who played board games?

Tutankhamun became pharaoh when he was only 12 years old. He loved playing a board game called senet, and after he died a board was buried with him in his tomb. It is a beautiful set, made of white ivory and a black wood called ebony.

● The senet board had 20 squares on one side and 30 on the other. Experts think it was a bit like ludo.

Did Egyptians like parties?

● Musicians plucked harps, beat drums and tambourines, blew pipes and shook tinkling bells.

The Egyptians might have spent a lot of time building tombs, but they weren't a miserable lot! They loved music and dancing. At rich people's banquets, there were often shows with dancing girls, musicians, acrobats and singers.

Why is paper called paper?

Our word 'paper' comes from papyrus, a tall reed that grows beside the Nile. The Egyptians discovered how to use the thready insides of these papyrus reeds to make a kind of paper. It was thicker than the paper we use today, but just as useful.

● Papyrus was expensive because it took so long to make. Quick notes were scribbled on pieces of pottery instead.

1 Paper-makers cut and peeled the reeds.

3 They hammered them until the sticky plant juices glued them together.

4 Next they used a smooth stone or a special tool to rub the surface of the papyrus paper smooth.

2 They cut the reed stems into thin slices and then laid them in rows, one on top of the other.

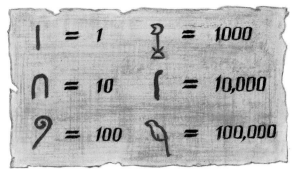

I = 1		= 1000	
∩ = 10		= 10,000	
= 100		= 100,000	

- Few children went to school. Some boys trained as scribes, people whose job was writing. They had to learn over 700 hieroglyphs. Spelling tests were a nightmare!

- There were even pictures for numbers. It can't have been easy doing sums!

What did Egyptian writing look like?

The first Egyptian writing was made up of rows of pictures, called hieroglyphs. Each picture stood for an object, an idea, or the sound of a word. Many of the hieroglyphs are quite complicated – they must have taken ages to draw!

- The ends of reeds were frayed to make paintbrushes. Ink was made from soot or red earth.

5 Finally, all the pieces of papyrus paper were glued into a long strip and rolled into a scroll.

- These hieroglyphs make up the name CLEOPATRA. Perhaps you can work out how to write TOP CAT or TREACLE.

C L E O P A T R A

Which were the most dangerous animals?

Egypt wasn't always a safe place. Wild bulls and lions lived in the desert, while hungry crocodiles lurked in the river Nile. Many Egyptians enjoyed hunting these animals, even though they could be dangerous.

● Even hippo-hunting could be dangerous. An angry hippo could easily overturn one of the hunter's tiny boats.

● When it died, a pet dog was buried with its collar – all ready for a walk in the after-life!

Did people have pets?

Rich Egyptians had pets, just as we do today, and they loved them just as much. Most people settled for a dog or a cat, but people who really wanted to show off kept pet apes and monkeys.

● Today there are no lions or hippos left in Egypt. They are only found in countries far to the south. But Ancient Egyptians would still recognize birds such as the ibis and the hoopoe.

● The whole family went along on duck hunts. The birds were brought down by sticks, which were a bit like boomerangs – only they didn't come back!

● Ostriches were hunted for their large tail feathers. These were made into beautiful fans to keep rich people cool.

What did Egyptians call their cats?

The Egyptian word for cat was miw – a cross between a mew and a miaow! The Egyptians were probably the first to tame cats. They used them to catch mice in grain stores.

29

How can you become an Egyptologist?

Egyptologists are people who study Ancient Egypt. To become one, you need to learn all about the history of Egypt, and the things that have survived from that time. Reading books and visiting museums are the best ways to start.

● Howard Carter went to Egypt in 1892, and spent many years excavating Ancient Egyptian tombs. He made his most famous discovery in 1920 – the tomb of the boy-pharaoh Tutankhamun.

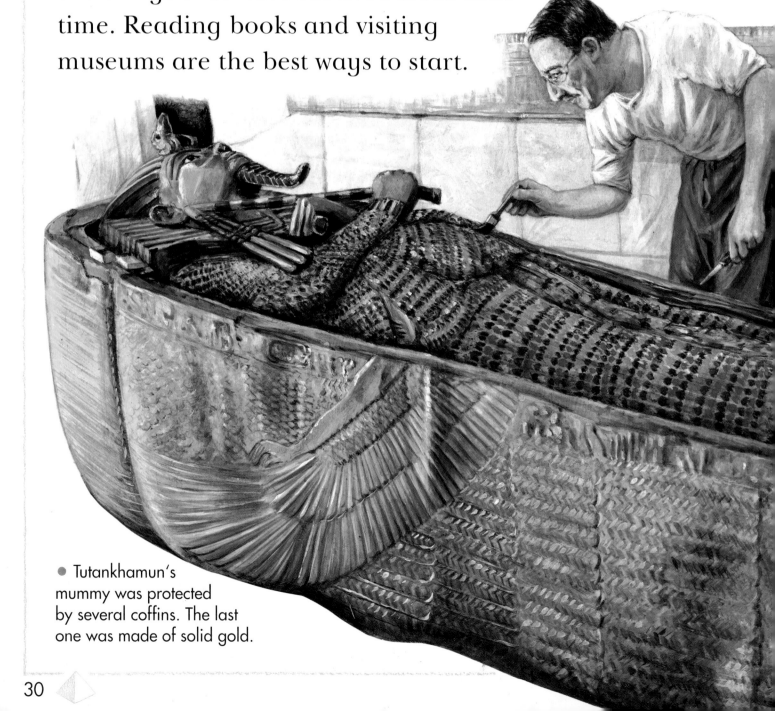

● Tutankhamun's mummy was protected by several coffins. The last one was made of solid gold.

Why do mummies have X-rays?

Modern science is a great help to Egyptologists. X-rays can show whether a mummy died from an illness or an accident. They can even tell whether it suffered from toothache!

● Egyptologists can even run tests on the things they find in a mummy's tummy, and work out what its last meal was before it died!

Where can you come face to face with a pharaoh?

Egypt's largest museum is in the capital city of Cairo. Here, you can gaze on the 4,000-year-old faces of the mummified pharaohs. Not all the pharaohs are here, though. Some are still lying peacefully, hidden in their desert tombs.

Index